I0132615

From the
CENTER

by
Sheldon Dillingham

PUBLISHING
Christian Literature & Artwork
A BOLD TRUTH Publication

From the CENTER
Copyright © 2016 Sheldon Dillingham

ISBN 13: 978-0-9972586-7-7

BOLD TRUTH PUBLISHING
Christian Literature & Artwork
300 West 41st
Sand Springs, Oklahoma 74063
www.BoldTruthPublishing.com
beirep@yahoo.com

Printed in the USA.

All rights reserved under International Copyright Law. All contents and/or cover art and design may not be reproduced in whole or in part in any form without the express written consent of the Author.

The views expressed in this book are not necessarily those of the publisher.

Contents

Acknowledgements

I want to thank the Lord Jesus Christ for pouring such grace on someone who is so undeserving. I know I am worthy, because he made me worthy. I did not earn such kindness, nevertheless I am not going to try to talk Him out of it. I also want to thank my wife for her patience and temperance while precious hours were spent doing the will of the Lord. I want to thank my daughter for her keen eyes and wonderful spiritual observation in helping proof the text and last but not least my publisher Aaron Jones, who is a great blessing to the body of Christ.

I want to thank you the reader ahead of time for implementing the valuable information immediately into your life. Be sure to pay close attention to chapter six and seven. The Lord chose to name this sixth chapter for a divine purpose.

Proverbs 4:23
Keep your heart with all diligence for out of it flow the issues of life.

I like to say it this way: Carefully guard the center for therein lays your day to day existence.

Sheldon D Dillingham

Preface

Concerning how I chose the book cover. I felt a timely key to living life FROM THE CENTER reminded me of a vision I experienced in 1996 while pondering a very important journey The Lord was desiring my family and I to embark on. It involved moving to another state and I was to attend a Bible College there; (which unbeknownst to us would totally rearrange our lives forever!) I was sitting in our home church one Sunday morning, I had it in my heart to ask The Lord why He wanted me to up root my family and go to this Bible College?

Suddenly I saw an old rugged altar, it had a stone slab laid across two stone legs. It looked like something you would see in a medieval movie. Laying across the altar was a extraordinarily beautiful woman, she had little to no clothing on her perfectly figured body, her eyes and lips were seductive and sensually alluring to me, in front of her was a computer screen, (I am sad to say has become one of peoples substitute of God in their lives,) and beside the computer screen was several stacks of money approximately 12 inches in height. As I gazed at the beautiful woman and her alluring companions, without any notice a huge cross came from above and slammed down in the center of the altar, shattering the woman, the computer screen and the money too pieces. I was shocked beyond measure as the vision slowly faded away. Looking back on the Heavenly Vision I realized Christ wants to be all and will not settle for nothing less!!

Introduction

by Sheldon D Dillingham

For clarities sake I need to help you dismiss any ideas of this book From The Center being about living the middle road of Christianity but on the contrary! It is just the opposite, it is a book that is designed to help you find your purpose in life and stay there by maintaining a good relationship with Jesus Christ our Heavenly Father and the Holy Spirit, it was designed to open the spiritual heart and the mental heart of you the believer. To know that Jesus Christ most definitely wants to train us to have complete and total dominion over all that we think and do.

His center for the mental heart is...

2 Corinthians 10:5
Casting down imaginations and every high thing that exalteth itself against the knowledge of God, and bringing into captivity every thought to the obedience of Christ.

His center for the spiritual heart is...

1 Peter 5:6-8
Humble your spirit therefore under the mighty hand of God, that He may exalt you in due season by casting all your cares upon Him for He cares for you. Be sober be vigilant because your enemy the devil as a roaring lion walks about seeking those he may devour.

Chapter 1

The Origin of The Center

In 1988 I was attending a small church in the High Sierra of sunny southern California with my wife and two young children. We had a wonderful Evangelist, Sister S. Jones, ministering one night. Her testimony was years ago she was healed of incurable cancer in one of Brother O's tent meetings in Australia. The healing even made front page news in her town.

She said the Lord had called her to preach His Word when He healed her, and she did just that. She was a very gifted and anointed preacher, as well as a beautiful saint; my wife and I loved her dearly.

I vividly remember on one of the nights during the meeting, (I remember so vividly) Sister Jones was preaching a fiery message. I was standing in the back of the church when she stopped preaching and walked back where I was. She grabbed me by the head and said, *"Take him to the throne of God!"*

The power of God struck my body with such force that I hit the floor. Suddenly! There He was! The King, Jesus Christ was standing over me! His face shined like the noonday sun. I took one look at Him and bowed my head; I was on my knees with my hands raised high. He said, *"I will take you before kings, kingdoms, nations and peoples."*

As He was talking, I looked behind me to see who He was talking to, I thought to myself, "Surely He is not talking to me!" Then He placed His left hand in my right hand and said, *"In times past you have felt my anointing in your left hand and now you will feel my anointing in your right hand."* I fell to the floor and began to weep. I asked, *"Lord how do I overcome pride?"* He answered, *"Use my wisdom! When you use my wisdom it will always overcome pride!"*

The authority in His voice was sweet, yet earth moving. He caused me to remember an incident that happened earlier that week and how the Holy Ghost led me out of a prideful snare of the devil by using the Lord's wisdom. I was expecting the power the Lord spoke of to show up in my right hand immediately; however, it happened ten days later. It is interesting how our time-related seasons here on earth are different than time-related seasons in the spirit.

I was worshiping the Lord in a Sunday morning service one day, when great power rose out of my spirit through my right hand, just as He had promised. I felt ten feet tall and bullet-proof when the electrifying anointing of the Lord flowed through my right hand.

It really is funny how it all happened. One minute I did not feel a thing and then, just seconds later, great power surged through me unlike anything I have ever felt before. It was a wonderful feeling that is difficult to describe with words.

As the years went on I realized something amazing had happen to me. For the first time in my Christian walk, I had truly felt like I was centered in line with God's plan for me. Even though I did not follow His plan perfectly and He still has to redirect me from time to time, it was the beginning of a centered, focused life for me.

All things must originate from the center in order to maintain a proportional design. The side of the North (where God resides), which is in the third heaven, pivots from the center of the universe. This is how He always has a perfect view of His creation. The passage you are about to read was quoted by the prophet Isaiah and inspired by the Spirit of God. Isaiah 14:13 states,

"For thou hast said in thine heart, I will ascend into heaven, I will exalt my throne above the stars of God: I will sit also upon the mount of the congregation, in the "sides of the north."

In this next passage some believe the character being quoted is satan or Lucifer before the fall. Isaiah 14:14 states,

"I will ascend above the heights of the clouds; I will be like the most High."

Years ago I had worked as a design draftsman. I was taught that before anything is drawn up or designed there must be a center line placed on the board as a point of symmetry. Only then can a picture be displayed or created in the proper balance. When God created all things He started from the center. God also created man to have a center place. This is the place where God can put His Word or laws so that He and man may have open communication.

In the beginning God would call Adam and Eve in the cool of the day to commune with him. I could always imagine Him meeting with them at the Tree of Life, which was located in the middle of the garden according to Revelations 2:7

"...I give to eat of the tree of life, which is in the midst of the paradise of God."

It is also interesting to note that this same tree represented the central existence for their (Adam and Eve) bodies. God designed the body to be sustained by the yield of the earth and Adam and Eve ate from the Tree of Life regularly it was to give their bodies eternal life.

This is made clear by the statement God made when He drove Adam and Eve out of the garden after they had sinned. In *Genius 3:22 God said"…lest he put his hand, and take also of the tree, and eat and live forever."* Now notice the phrase "live forever". We know He could not be talking about life of the spirit or soul because these died the moment they ate of the Tree of the Knowledge of Good and Evil.

> *"But of the tree of the knowledge of good and evil, you will not eat of it: for in the day that thou eat there of you will surely die" Genesis 2:17*

Therefore it is obvious He was not only speaking of death of the spirit and soul but death of the human body also. In His great mercy He did not want them to live in their human bodies forever by eating from the Tree of Life. The Tree of Life would have sustained their human bodies forever; however, their soul and spirit would have been dead. God was sparing Adam and Eve from a life of hell on earth, trapped inside their bodies while death reigned in their spirit and soul. God knew redemption was coming for their spirit, soul, and a new body was on the way through Jesus Christ's death, burial and resurrection! I Corinthians 15:52 states,

> *"In a moment, in the twinkling of an eye, at the last trump: for the trumpet shall sound, and the dead shall be raised incorruptible, and we shall be changed."*

God's original purpose for the Tree of Life was to sustain them in paradise where they could live and walk with Him forever. He would call to meet with them in the cool of the day and, I truly believe, it was to build a relationship with His people and discuss the plans and provisions He had for their lives. Equally important were their conversations concerning His creation and what they enjoyed most in it. God has glorious plans for His people. Even in the mess that man has created He still has a marvelous plan to bring everything into fruition.

Have you ever heard a sermon and the preacher seemed as though he was preaching directly to you? Or maybe you picked up the Bible and the page opens to the spiritual food you need for the day. Perhaps you got a feeling on the inside that He is trying to speak to you, but you think it is just your head. That is God calling you from the center to fellowship with you.

He is constantly looking for opportunities to prove that He is thinking of you. It is the three of them (the Father, Son, and Holy Spirit) calling you to discuss what is lodged in your heart. Here are some people who experienced this with Jesus after His resurrection. Look here at Luke 24:32,

"And they said one to another, Did not our heart burn within us, while he talked with us by the way, and while he opened to us the scriptures?"

That burning effect was their spirits responding to His call from the center. He said in *John 10:27 "My sheep hear my voice, and I know them, and they follow me."* So when you feel that tug on your heart, yield to it and say, "Okay, Father. I desire to line up with Your word." Then He will begin to examine your heart, to see how much value you place on His Word by measuring it from the center of your life.

As a draftsman I learned that the further from the center I got when I was drawing, the more the picture was distorted. It is same with the Word of God in the mind portion of your heart and the spirit portion of your heart. When I say "heart" I am referring to the center and core of your spirit, soul, and body. Your heart is a vast spiritual organism that evaluates your every movement.

The spirit of man is the candle of the LORD, searching all the inward parts of the belly. Proverbs 20:27

Notice the spirit is different from the inward parts of the belly? The Strong's Exhaustive Concordance of the Bible describes this word "belly" to mean "hallow." the word "inward" means "chamber" and the word "parts" means "divide or cut out." The heart resides in a cut-out hallow part in the center of your spirit. There are many chambers in it.

Let's look at a person in Scripture. Notice what they allowed in the spiritual and mental portion of the heart, and how it too acted out in their body. Job 20:19-20 says,

"Because he (the spirit and mental man) has oppressed and hath forsaken the poor; because he (the spirit and mental man) hath violently taken away a house which he built not; Surely he (the spirit and mental man) shall not feel quietness in his belly, he shall not save of that which he desired.

Notice the words "has oppressed." This man decided the value of other humans is not as important as his. It's interesting the word describes him as a "oppressor." The definition of an "oppressor" is one who burdens with cruel or unjust impositions or restraints; subject to a burdensome or harsh exercise of authority or power. These acts are done with planning of the spirit and mind in the heart.

Let's look a little closer at this guy. Notice the word "forsaken." According to Strong's a better rendering of this word is "destitute" is to cause someone to be destitute of food, clothing and shelter is a premediated act of the spirit and soul of a person in the heart. This man is violent which takes the spirit, soul and body to do.

All these acts are done from the heart. Because God put His law in our heart we cannot do evil without it dealing with us to the same degree as we deal it out. I am referring to the heart as a organ that has the capacity to store good and evil, and the only one that can guide it is you. This word "belly" is the same word previously mentioned in Job 19. This hallow place is the housing of the heart. Look at the word "save." Strong's describes it as meaning "to escape by slipperiness." In other words judgement day is coming, pal!

The way Strong's translates this word reminds me of a Christian camp in the mountain of one of our beautiful forests here in America. Somewhere people paid hard-earned money to turn in their cell phones and all electronic devices so they could sit and listen to nature. However, the camp ran into a small snag and that was the things people had in their spiritual belly (where heart resides). Many cases, people were running down the mountain trying to escape the darkness they buried deep within their heart. They thought these issues were gone far from them. They felt by spending more time on their devices and with brother Google 'god-on-our-globe-leading-everyone,' God would not take the opportunity to bring up many deep seated issues that were push aside and masked over by device addictions. No matter how fast they run or how far they went they had one huge problem! They were carrying their spiritual heart with them.

You see, like most of society today devices are not only used for communication or for conveniences, it is also used to drown out people and the way we treat them. Jesus wants us to put down the devices and take up your neighbor's cause which quite honestly is inconvenience and time consuming but there is no greater reward and cure for the spiritual belly pain a lot of people are going through today.

Proverbs 23:7 says, *"For as he thinks in his heart, so is he."*

When God speaks to a person, saved or unsaved, He is speaking to their central belief system. God is a quickening Spirit, He has total access to your spirit if you are a believer, but limited access to your dead soul. This is by His own doing. When He created us He did not want robots but a family like Him. God will guide your soul through His Word if you are willing to yield to it. It is through His word that He gains full access to your soul. That's why He says to renew your soul or mind in *Romans 12:2*

And be not conformed to this world: but be ye transformed by the renewing of your mind, that ye may prove what is that good, and acceptable, and perfect, will of God .

So let me say again, there are three areas designated in the heart that are designed from the original creation, spiritual, mental and body.

And the very God of peace sanctify you wholly; and

I pray God your whole spirit and soul and body be preserved blameless unto the coming of our Lord Jesus Christ. 1 Thessalonians 5:23

This passage is using the word "blameless" which is a spiritual belly phrase. This is important because when you are studying the word so you may differentiate between the three. It is also important to note when you are cross-referencing the word "heart" in the Old Testament. If you take the time to read the whole passage, you will find the majority of the references are dealing with the soul which are the mind, will and emotions. However, when you cross over to the New Testament, the word "heart" is more often than not, dealing with the spirit.

So in the beginning the first Adam was a living soul because Jesus had not yet died and rose from the dead for our justification. Therefore, his spirit could not have been born again. The last Adam, which is Christ, is a quickening Spirit according to

1 Corinthians 15:45. and so it is written, The first man Adam was made a living soul; the last Adam was made a quickening spirit.

We must always remember concerning creation that God's perspective revolves and evolves around one central truth. We find this central truth in the book of Colossians 1:16

"For by him (Jesus) all things were created, that are in heaven, and that in the earth, visible and invisible, whether they be thrones, or dominions, or principalities, or powers: all things were created by Him, And for Him: and He (Jesus) is before all things, and by Him all things consist."

When we as believers begin to grasp this truth it will cause us to receive Him in the fullness of who He is. Then His word will bring a new light to your spirit, soul and body and the life of God's Word will cause a quickening effect within you. If you will allow this evolution process to take root, the affect will catapult you far ahead of anything contrary to His Word. When the word is operating in a fuller dimension in your life, it can do in us what it is meant to do within you. Hebrews 4:12 states,

"For the word of God is quick, and powerful, and sharper than any two edged sword, piercing even to the dividing asunder of soul and spirit, and of the joints and marrow (the body), and is a discerner of the thoughts and intents of the heart."

Chapter 2
Recognize Your Center

Take this journey with me into what the Bible calls the "hidden man of the heart."

"But let it be the hidden man of the heart, in that which is not corruptible, even the ornament of a meek and quiet spirit, which is in the sight of God of great price." 1 Peter 3:4

Notice this verse does not say hidden man "is" the heart but "of" the heart. Some say the spirit is the heart and I can understand the method of how they arrived at that conclusion. They are closely related and they both are spiritual but, it is important to separate the two because the spirit is not in the heart (just like your outer physical body is not in your physical heart). The heart is located in the belly of our spirit. This may come as a surprise, God the Creator possess a heart. Here's a thought. If God is a Spirit and His Spirit is His heart then who is "His" referred to in Genesis 8:21 "the Lord said in His heart". This statement tells us God possess a heart. He is not a heart! His heart is located in His belly area like He created us.

"He that believeth on me, as the scripture hath said, out of his belly shall flow rivers of living water (but this

Jesus spoke of the Spirit), which they that believed on him would receive: for the Holy Spirit had not been given: because Jesus had not been glorified yet". John 7:38 -39

So you see the Spirit is located in our belly the hallow part where the heart resides. To prove my point here's a little test you can take. The next time you are convicted or guided by the Holy Spirit pay attention to where this stirring comes from. You will notice it comes from your belly area. The heart is a spiritual organ and we are going to look closely at this entity to know what it is and why it was designed by our Heavenly Father.

First what it is: the word "man" in the Scripture (1 Peter 3:4) is a generic term because it is not gender oriented. Although a gender may be applied to this word it literally means "human being" or "person." In other words, the hidden person of the heart. God is always moving to help His children find the center of His will. This is the place where His Word should reside. When the Eternal Evaluator of Hearts asks us a question He is not looking for information. He's trying to help us recognize the center.

We find a classic example of this with in the Garden of Eden. God asked Eve a question in Genesis 3:13:

"And the LORD God said unto the woman, what is this that thou hast done? And the woman said, the serpent beguiled me, and I did eat."

God asked Eve what she had done as an act of mercy, so she would know His word still held a position in her heart. Now instead of being in the center of what once was a beautiful living soul (I say "living soul" because the Scriptures say in

1 Corinthians 15:45 - And so it is written. The first man Adam was made a "living soul") was a dead spirit and soul. Because of His act mercy, she immediately recognized God's law had been tampered with and replaced from her center. She put it back into proper position so that she might communicate with the living God.

How do we know this? Because she said, "The serpent lied to me and I did eat." If she was still in her deceived state she would have said, "That serpent you created told me I would have knowledge of good and evil so I ate." God wanted her to know His Word had the ability to unite with her dead spirit and soul, which brought her back to the center.

I imagine Eve must have recognized the problem when fear took hold of her and the love of the Creator was no longer the center of her will. She must have thought about His question for many years after they were removed from the garden, God has asked us many questions in our lifetime. The truth is we must know our Heavenly Father does not ask questions for information, but so that we may recognize our current position from the center. He does this so that we may evaluate our own hearts with making decisions in this life. We can choose to stay off course or move back to the center where we belong. So the question is how do we get back to the center once we recognize we are off course?

Jesus said it best when He gave the analogy of the farmer in Matthew 13:3-9:

"And he spoke many things unto them in parables, saying, Behold, a sower went forth to sow; And when he sowed, some seeds fell by the way side, and the fowls came and devoured them up: Some fell upon stony plac-

es, where they had not much earth: and forthwith they sprung up, because they had no depth of earth: And when the sun was up, they were scorched; and because they had no root, they withered away. And some fell among thorns; and the thorns sprung up, and choked them: But other fell into good ground, and brought forth fruit, some a hundredfold, some sixtyfold, some thirtyfold."

I refer to these as the six conditions of the spirit and soul of the human heart. This gives an accurate measurement of how far from the center each person was except one. For an example, the fourth person was right on center producing a hundred fold. Both the fifth and sixth person produced, but not as much as they could have.

Another thing I find rather interesting, which we will discuss in later chapters is that the number six is the Lord's number for man. As the sower sowed it was completely up to the prepared heart to receive what was sown. It is also interesting to note that the three prepared hearts had one thing in common and that was they received the sown word in a measure on good ground. After close observation, and considering the thousands of people I have ministered to over the last thirty years, I have not found anyone outside of these six conditions. It is also important to note that the heart (the ground) that produces thirty-fold still had seventy-fold of one of the other poor conditions of the heart in operation. The same is true for the heart that had sixty-fold which had forty-fold of the poor conditions of the heart in operation.

Each of these numbers represent how far off from the center of God's will they were. The three Jesus did not put a value on were prospects for God's mercy to develop, just as the others. Look at how Jesus described each person's individual ability to keep God's Word in the center of their own heart.

You see, the level of personal connection to God's center is solely dependent upon a person's ability to receive and walk in His word; Jesus is not giving out free passes. He fully expects all people to hook and run with His teaching. Now let's look a little closer at Eve's response to our Heavenly Father's question again.

Remember, Eve is desperately trying to bring all things back to the center at our Heavenly Father's request. Her first move was recognizing her current position. This was the only way she could genuinely answer the question. Keep in mind every word she spoke was from the origin or center of her heart. Eve had no way of searching inward for some kind of ancient philosophy, because it was not available. There was no point of reference she could turn too. First of all, she has never heard or seen anyone in this predicament before. Secondly, she had no inward witness to guide her. Each word she chose had to be chosen carefully. This was to ensure her return to the center, so she could find herself in alignment with the living God.

It is clear that no man or woman after Adam and Eve ever had to deal with speaking from such an origin related position before. The Word says that three elements must come into play before we find ourselves centered properly. They can be found in *1 John 2:16*,

"For all that is in the world, the lust of the flesh, and the, lust of the eyes, and the pride of life, is not of the Father, but is of the world."

The first is a strong craving of the flesh. The second is the lust of the eyes. The third is pride of self-sufficiency. Though Eve was deceived in all three of these areas, her keen spiritual awareness gave a full description of the devil's handiwork. When she answered God by saying "the serpent beguiled me," it was very clear to her: the father of lies and seduction blinded her. Here's how the scripture descripts satan's maniacal workings.

"In whom the god of this world hath blinded the minds of them which believe not, lest the light of the glorious gospel of Christ, who is the image of God, should shine unto them." 2 Corinthians 4:4

So this is another subtlety that gives us insight into Eve's dealing with satan.

Now the word "beguiled" is an Old English word used in the Greek and Hebrew. This word in its true context does not mean "deceived" or "lied to" in the more common sense. Rather it is deception by a form of hypnotic seduction, and it is one of the strongest types of deception. This word carries a deeper root of seduction beyond one's ability to control or stop if you're willing to go down its devious road. Once someone travels down this elusive trail with this dark being, their spirit and soul have been manipulated many times beyond repair. Let us elaborate on this story a little more.

It reminds me of an experience I once had in dealing with satan and his hypnotic seduction. It was during an intense battle with spiritual wickedness in heavenly places that went on for months. I was at the end of my rope and completely exhausted when I cried unto the Lord for the third or fourth time. He replied to me, "I will give you satan." I was not sure what that meant but then he begin to download a series of words and Scriptures to help me fight the battle.

As I repeated what I heard Him say, suddenly I heard an evil voice speaking to me with overwhelming authority. It startled me, yet it seemed to be coming from within my soul: it was satan himself. The Lord explained to me that the connection I was experiencing was dead soul to dead soul. Satan is not the author of evil, he is a partaker of evil. Jesus called him the Father of Lies and if you look carefully you will see how he fell from the center.

"You are of your father the devil, and the lusts of your father you will do. He was a murderer from the beginning, and abode not in the truth, because there is no truth in him. When he speaks a lie, he speaks of his own: for he is a liar, and the father of it." John 8:44

When I spoke the words God gave me, it pierced him deeply. Then Satan simply responded to me saying, "Things were different then." The truth is that it was not his reply that shook me. It was his ability to make his words pulsate in my soul like throbbing pain in your body when you strike your knee or hit your thumb with a hammer. The words were so deeply hypnotic and seductive I knew if it were not for the power God and His anointing present in this encounter I would have easily believed his lies.

One portion in Disney's "The Jungle Book," if you have ever seen the movie you'll remember, there is a scene when the serpent, who when it was approached by someone, would begin to sing. While he is singing, a hypnotic enticement would happen with his eyes and his audience would suddenly become prey to his seduction.

In the movie there is also a tiger that knew the jungle well and roamed around without fear because he knew every weakness of every animal that lived there. When the serpent tried to hypnotize him, the tiger simply stomped his head underneath his paw, telling him to "stop that nonsense."

I often imagined the serpent to be Satan and the tiger to be the Holy Spirit in that analogy. As believers following the Holy Spirit we can slam the devil on the head and say, "Stop that nonsense!" Glory to God!

After this encounter I had with the Deceiver himself. The Holy Spirit said to me, "That is how he deceived Eve." I began to understand Eve's fall a bit differently. I changed my focus to how he used seductive manipulation to draw Eve from the center. Notice in the previously mentioned passage Jesus said "and abode not in the truth." The word abode means "covenant" so in other words Jesus said he broke covenant from the truth. In doing so he died and his soul was no longer alive.

Let's look at this passage carefully, *1 John 3:15* says, *"you know that no murderer hath eternal life abiding in him."* So this dead creature was after one thing in that garden and one thing only; to murder these to innocent living souls. This idea is so far from the center and the purpose for which he was created as one could possibly get.

So you see, my beloved of God, when Satan comes, it is to move you from the center of your Creator's plan for your life. Simply focus on the word of God, tell him "no," and take your position with the word on your lips standing alongside your heavenly Father who is so much greater for us then any evil that can be against us!

God, our heavenly Father wants you to know the word 'Satan' means "adversary." The original word is "saw-tan" which means "to attack," but Satan does not just attack once and it's over. He will continually pound at you, and pound at you, until he can get you away from the center. Even then he will pound more. Saints, do not be quiet. Have faith in God's word. Keep your focus straight and clear so that you may be an effective tool for Lord at all times.

Chapter 3
The Door to The Center

In order to understand the door to a person's heart we must first look closer at the heart. We touched on this in the first two chapters; however, we are now going to go deeper into this very difficult subject.

In the Old Testament writings you will find the word "heart" is often associated with the mind or will of a person. This makes perfect sense seeing that Adam and Eve were living souls or minds. However, in the New Testament you will find the word "heart" being closely related to the spirit of a person since under the New Testament we are recreated as quickening spirits. What is clear is that the heart is a "spiritual processor."

It processes only what it is given through the physical, mental and spiritual senses and produces it into what we call "believing." Jesus warns us to be careful of how we allow seeds from the affairs of life to enter in our processor. He used the parable of the Kingdom to get this point across. *Mark 4:24* says,

> *"and He (Jesus) said unto them, Take heed what ye hear: with what measure ye measure it, it shall be measured to you: and unto you that hear shall more be given."*

In looking at this revolutionary statement I find turning off our religious heads for a while is the only way we can understand the process the heart goes through. Let me explain.

Jesus did not say if you are a Christian that measures things right God will give you more to measure. Jesus said (if you will allow me to para phase) that if you put anything in your heart the processing mechanism will begin producing it inside of you.

This statement applies to every human being believers and nonbelievers alike. This is a simple part that many people misunderstand. Jesus had not yet died on the cross; therefore, He was speaking to those who were dead in spirit and soul. So, the increase and decrease application of the heart is already built inside of us and that is how we are all wired. I call this the "process of believing".

It makes no difference what you put in your heart. The more you feed it, the more it will produce. The less you feed it, the less it will produce. This will continue until it is either producing greatly for God's Kingdom or nothing at all for God's Kingdom. The danger, or the "take heed" He is referring to, is how you measure or evaluate what you hear.

We are going to take a look at *Mark 4:24-29*. In these verses Jesus is using the words the "Kingdom of God" and "earth." However, as an example, I am going to briefly change the words "Kingdom of God" to "heart processing mechanism" and the word "earth" to "heart" so you can easily see how the process works. Look closer with me in *Mark 4:24-29*:

> *"and he said unto them, Take heed what ye hear: with what measure you measure it, it shall be measured to you: and unto you that hear shall more be given. For he that hath, to him shall be given: and he that hath not, from him shall be taken even that which he hath. And he said, so is the kingdom of God (heart processing mech-*

anism), as if a man should cast seed into the ground (heart); And should sleep, and rise night and day, and the seed should spring and grow up, he knows not how. For the earth (heart) brings forth fruit of herself; first the blade, then the ear, after that the full corn in the ear. But when the fruit is brought forth, immediately he puts in the sickle, because the harvest is come"

It is important to note Jesus is referencing to the Kingdom of God because that is where this process came from. It is a spiritual process; not physical.

So many misguided people have found themselves overwhelmed simply because they had no idea what they were putting in this processing system call the "heart". I do find it funny, however, that many people today want to put Jesus's teaching in this mystical, and even unqualified place in their heart as many religious people of His day did. They somehow think that only the great theologians carry a clear understanding of such a deep subject. Nevertheless, I believe the Creator of this system has more than enough credentials for me.

If we listen and do what He says evil will not be the lord over our lives and we will find grace to win the way our Heavenly Father desires us to.

God tells us to diligently guard our heart, yet, so few know of its natural processing system. They are aware that their lives are being dictated and governed by something supernatural and designed to lead them through life by the decisions they make or that others are making for them.

The mystery of it all is why people want to believe one thing in their processor and expect something totally different to be at their door. They (the people of Yesuha's day) could never listen to the teachings of Jesus from a living prospective because these people were both in spiritually and mentally dead. This includes the Jews along with all the nations of the earth at that time.

So many of the statements Jesus made pertained to all peoples and not only those who were under the Abrahamic covenant. If we understand this truth it will be easier to see people the way He sees them. We will begin to see why our Father has such intense grace through compassion instead of judgement.

It reminds me of a time I was attending a church in southern California. Our pastor had announced that our music leader and his wife were leaving and were starting another church many miles away from our church. We were all very excited for them. However, after hearing through the grapevine, we found out this music leader and his wife were starting a church in the neighboring city which was only a few miles away. I could hear the pain in my pastor's voice when he announced this very dear friend of his lied to him and broke his heart. He and his wife held their composure extremely well in light of the circumstances, because of the love they had for the congregation.

I was younger in my walk with the Lord at the time so I got very upset and I mourned all the way home. When I got there (home), I fell on my knees and cried out to the Living God. I was so infuriated by this music leader and his wife. All of our congregation knew how good our pastor and his wife had been to this brother and sister in the Lord, and how he and his wife grew up spiritually with them. After all, they had been friends with our pastor for over twenty years. They flourished under a very powerful man and woman of God and came out of that church together. Bottom line was that this music minister and his wife knew better and it hurt deeply.

As I anguished over this situation before the Lord, I was

ready to call fire down on them and consume them in a second. While I was praying, a deep groaning and travail concerning the matter came over me. God's power fell on me and suddenly I was in the Spirit. I could feel our Heavenly Father's heart concerning this matter. He too was very hurt.

While I was in the spirit I saw two thrones. I knew one was a judgement seat and the other was the Mercy seat of Christ. I could not tell you how I knew that because there were no signs above either throne. I just knew in my spirit which was which. I ran to the judgement throne with all my might. I could feel the anger, rage and hurt coursing through my spiritual veins like a volcano ready to irrupt. Then all at once an arm and hand swooped me up and brought me to the mercy seat. As I wept bitterly in His arms He said, "We don't do that to our own."

I still do not fully understand what he meant by that, but His words went through me like a cool breeze on a hot summer's day and my soul was filled with love. While He was healing me, I could not see anything but a glorious light all around me. Through this light I saw how Jesus controlled His emotions by using His gracious love and compassion. I was highly impressed. I could speak nothing else but blessings from that seat of grace and mercy for my brother and sister (the music minister and his wife) with all my heart.

I learned two valuable lessons about the mental portion of the heart that day. The first thing I learned was our heart will run as hard and as fast towards any open door you allow it to. The second thing I learned was the heart (the mental portion of the heart) can be healed through the power of the cross and the stripes of our Savior. You see, my peace was being chastised and according to *Isaiah 53:5*, Jesus paid the price so that I could be free of that. *Isaiah 53:5* states,

"But he was wounded for our transgressions, he was bruised for our iniquities: the chastisement of our peace was upon him; and with his stripes we are healed."

Though our hearts may be repaired it is absolutely imperative that we do not allow the door of heart to be easily opened to the persuasion of our emotions, outer influences, and even our own thoughts if they are contrary to what the word of God says. One may ask, where is the door to the heart? Let's look at *Genesis 4:7,*

"If thou does well (or does what I tell you to do), shalt thou be accepted? And if thou does not well, sin lie at the door. And unto thee shall be his desire, and thou shalt rule over him."

Some believe, the phrase "sin lies at the door" is a metaphor; however, the words used are very literal. God was making the law of sin and death clear when He said these Words.

This is a good time to mention the heart as a processing mechanism to better clarify this point. Such knowledge had not yet been exposed concerning the heart, or the heart as a processing mechanism, if you will. In essence, we must get a hold of what our heart is processing in order to keep evil from entering in and eventually leading to death in the most in important areas of life such as our health, family, friends, money, etc. I have a painfully honest truth for you and it is this: sin is always at the door of our dead soul. Paul said in *Romans 7:21 "I find then a law, that, when I would do good, evil is present with me."*

So in order to keep sin out we must take God's Word and guard the door. His promises are designed to made us feel and look like kings. The door is like a gate that swings both ways, and the gate is located in the mind and spirit portion of the heart. Just like our mouth is used to eat natural healthy foods, and it can also be used to eat processed unhealthy foods. The door to our soul (mind, will and emotions) and spirit can either be fed things that will make them weak or things that will build them up. Cain failed to diligently protect the door to his heart. This allowed envy in and envy invited murder to join the party.

Here is another interesting use of this word "door." In *Revelations 3:20* Jesus says, *"I stand at the door and knock…"* It is intriguing that Jesus would use such a statement seeing that He was already in those people's heart. What door was Jesus referring to? What place was Jesus having to knock to get into?

When we look at the physical heart we find there are valves leading to different areas in the heart. It is the same with the spiritual, mental and physical portion of the heart. There are chambers and doors to open and close.

Jesus is in the center of the spiritual portion of the heart of His siblings, however He is a foreigner to the mental portion of the heart therefore He must ask for access. In order for Jesus to have access to this area we must invite Him by renewing our mind so that we might see and understand, without a doubt what God's perfect will is for our lives. Remember God's regeneration plan does involve the soul/mind until we get our new bodies. It is groan for that day. The process is revolutionary!

Psalms 24:7 Lift up your heads, O ye gates; and be ye lift up, ye everlasting doors; and the King of glory shall come in. Who is this King of glory? The Lord strong and mighty, the Lord in battle. Lift up your heads, O ye gates; even lift them up, ye everlasting doors; and the King of glory? Who is this King of glory? The Lord of hosts, he is the King of glory. Selah.

The gates represent the dungeon gates of the law of sin and death on many levels, to name a couple. One of the first is the gates of hell mentioned my Yeshua to Peter when He revealed the power of the redeemed Church, His body. Another was how it all took place as He took captivity captive and gave gifts unto His body through the grace of the Holy Spirit. Which leads us to *Psalms 24:7-10.* When God through the work of the Holy Spirit sets people free, the gates are lifted up and Christ is able to enter the of the dead spirit of any willing person who excepts His transforming grace. *Ephesians 2:8 for by grace are you saved through faith: it is the gift of God:*

Christ took center place as "King of Glory" which once was occupied by the law of sin and death.

Romans 8:3 for what the law could not do, in that it was weak through the flesh, God sending His own Son in the likeness of sinful flesh, and for sin in the flesh:

The Word of God said it well when *Psalms 24:7* echo "King of Glory". When Christ enters the heart of a person commanding the gates/doors to open and the transformation is taking place in that person's spirit, that dead soul is crying out. Who is the "King of Glory"? While the spirit is being transformed (God is creating a new person) Christ is proclaiming who He is to that dead soul, also to the law of sin and death "the Lord strong and mighty the Lord mighty in battle". Our dead soul longs to be part of the regeneration process so, it asked again. Who is the "King of Glory"? the Lord replies "the Lord of hosts, He is the "King of Glory". However we can help our non-regenerated soul walk in unity with our regenerated spirit by performing the procedure in *Romans 12: 1-3.* When this is done the door to the soul will be open wide for His Spirit to operate through us. It is essential for the believer to leave the door unguarded to the Holy Spirit!

"I beseech you therefore, brethren, by the mercies of God, that ye present your bodies a living sacrifice, holy, acceptable unto God, which is your reasonable service. And be not conformed to this world: but be ye transformed by the renewing of your mind, that ye may prove what is that good, acceptable and perfect will of God." Romans 12:1-3

This mind renewing process is like tilling the ground of the soul in our hearts for the fresh seed of God's Word to be planted. It is a continual process. A soul that is not continually being renewed is very weak as the prophet Jeremiah so clearly puts it in *Jeremiah 17:9:*

"The heart is deceitful above all things, and desperately wicked: who can know it?"

His assessment of the dead soul portion of the heart is very clear and accurate. That's why God calls it His enemy. Another good Scripture we can reference is *2 Corinthians 10:5* which states,

"Casting down imaginations, and every high thing that exalts itself against the knowledge of God, and bringing into captivity every thought to the obedience of Christ."

Thank God He did not leave us without options! Through our Lord and Savior we are commanded to control this un-purified mind by the *"casting down of imaginations" and by the "washing of the water of the word" (Ephesians 5:26 that He might sanctify and cleanse it).*

I know this passage is referring to what Christ does for the church, however we can follow His example and use this same process to purify our minds. I have done it on many occasions by mediating on God's word day and night. The word mediate means to "murmur." Jesus said His Word is "spirit and life." It only takes a small portion of the seed of the word in a fertile mind to cause us to hear and yield more clearly to what the Spirit is saying from the center. Nevertheless, it is a battle and a battle well fought can only bring victory in Jesus name!

When Jesus was speaking of standing at the door of our hearts in *Revelation 3:20,* the evidence that we are allowing the door of our hearts to be opened or closed is the doing of our Fathers will or not. Often times we become so centered on the cares of this world that we allow other things to crowd Jesus out. When we crowd Him out of the soul portion of our hearts we lose our only true source of life.

Jesus says in *John 14:6* that He is the way the truth and the life. He is establishing himself as one of the foundational parts in all of creation. "The Amen" which means "so be it!" He is "The Faithful" which means "dependable" or "ironclad." He is The True Witness," which means "the one whose testimony is pure true." He is "The Beginning of Creation of God" which means "the original Center of Creation! Glory be to God! So let's go back to Jesus knocking at the door of the soul portion of our heart.

Jesus not only weighs a man's heart by its transparency, but

He also weighs our works. In Revelation 2 Jesus states "I know thy works," twice, both in verse 2 and verse 9. This is an evaluation statement. So when Jesus weighs the works (motives and passion by which we perform our works), He looks to see if our heart by which we performs those works is hot, cold, or neither. Why is it important to be hot or cold? Because when a person is lukewarm he is lost in his passion for anything. Jesus can work with cold. Believe it or not, Saul, who after his conversion became the Apostle Paul, is a classic example of a cold prospect for the Lord to work with.

> "And Saul, yet breathing out threats and slaughter against the disciples of the Lord, went unto the high priest, and desired of him letters to Damascus to the synagogues, that if he found any of this way, whether they were men or women, he might bring them bound unto Jerusalem." Acts 9:1

Now if you look closely at this open door to the center of Saul's cold heart, you will find it to be a perfect time for the Lord to show Saul how far off center he really was even though his passion for God was misguided. When I say "door" I'm referring to our Lord's accesses to our movements and plans in life.

It reminds me of a childhood game we used to play. We would hide an object and see if the other players could find it. Sometimes if the other player was getting close you gave a hint by saying "you are getting hotter," or if they were far away, you would say, "You're cold." However if you did not move, they would never find the object hidden. Then no hint would be necessary and, therefore, you would lose the game.

The Lord views a Christian that is not in motion as a candidate for losing at life. He does not want to confess a person who is halfheartedly living for him. That person will never taste the beauty of His confession to Our Heavenly Father and His glorious angels. Such a person that lacks passion, and is living a lukewarm life. The Bible say He will spit Him out of His mouth (Revelation 3:16). My brother and sister, passion for the "Amen" (Jesus Christ) of God is an uncompromising way of life for us. You may say "I am rich and have need of nothing." Being the True Witness that He is, He sees our wretched, miserable, poor, and blind state, and agrees with them. He tells us how we can become a true witness from the center like Him, and how we can walk in His purpose for our lives, which is of great importance. It is evident He knows the terrible condition of our dead soul because He is the Alpha and the Omega. He stands at door of a poor dead Christian soul and offers a priceless divine prescription.

I say "divine prescription for their death soul" because these Christians in *Revelations 3:16* were very fleshly and had compromised their spiritual heritage. They accepted fool's gold, as it were, to guide them from the center, pride of self-sufficiency and vain glory is a form of fool's gold in our Fathers eyes.

Children of the Most High God, we must always pay close attention to the center of our heart so that the life that pours out of us is of Him. We never want Him outside knocking on the door. He must have free accesses if we are to flow with His Spirit. When we choose to ignore our heart, our lives needlessly suffer the consequences.

I had a case once dealing with a young business man who called me and asked for prayer for his business. He said at first his business was really booming, then all of a sudden things went dry and he couldn't figure it out. I knew the answer was what he had allowed in his heart. I told him to go in the back of his shop and grab a bucket and sit on it and say, "Father, our business was booming and now we are experiencing dry bones what's going on?"

So as he sat there he heard from the center of his heart our Heavenly Father say, "Do you remember a few days ago when you placed a large order from your vendor? You made a mistake and ordered too many things. So to cover for yourself, when the young lady came to deliver your order you lied and said it was the wrong order because you were afraid the vendor would make you pay for it." "Yes," the young business man replied. Then the Lord said to him, "When you did that, you opened the door for Satan to erode your business and you also got the young lady who delivered your order in a lot of trouble and she was almost fired."

The young business man was telling me the story just as he remembered it. He then said to me I thought to myself "I've got to make this right," so he called the manager of that company he was doing business with and told him everything that had happened. He told him he would pay for the wrong order and the manager said he appreciated his honest and business and that he did not have to pay for the bad order. Then he went to the delivery company, apologized to the young lady and gave her a gift as well. After he did that, late that same day a mountain of business came in.

This story is only a small example of what God is willing to do for those who are willing to simply make a heart adjustment to move their desires to the side and come back to the center. Jesus had a case once dealing with a business man named Zacchaeus in *Luke 19:2-10*:

> *"And, behold, there was a man named Zacchaeus, which was the chief among the publicans, and he was*

rich. And he sought to see Jesus who he was; and could not for the press, because he was little of stature. And he ran before, and climbed up into a sycamore tree to see him: for he was to pass that way. And when Jesus came to the place, he looked up, and saw him, and said unto him, Zacchaeus, make haste, and come down; for today I must abide at thy house. And he made haste, and came down, and received him joyfully. And when they saw it, they all murmured, saying, that he was gone to be guest with a man that is a sinner. And Zacchaeus stood, and said unto the Lord; Behold, Lord, the half of my goods I give to the poor; and if I have taken anything from any man by false accusation, I restore him fourfold. And Jesus said unto him, This day is salvation come to this house, for so much as he also is a son of Abraham. For the Son of man is come to seek and to save that which was lost."

We can gather from Jesus' last statement that the center purpose of His coming was to seek and save the lost, bring them back, and open their eyes to the heart and direction of the Father. Notice the attitude of this chief publican was "joy" when Jesus said he was coming to his house. This is a attitude of honor and respect towards God. Honor and respect are two vital ingredients in paving the road back to the center of God's will for your life.

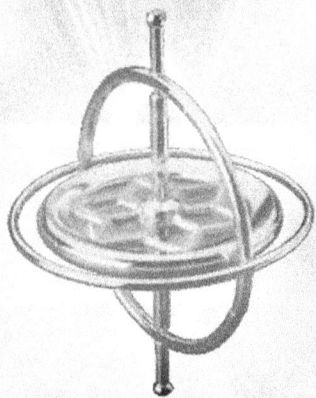

Chapter 4

God has Everything on a Positional Pivot

What is a positional pivot? It is the center point from where all creation aligns itself. God may have you give your neighbor a bag of groceries and it may be the neighbor that hates you and your old religion. So you say to the Lord, "Lord, this person hates us. Are you sure?" And the answer is yes! What you don't know is, this very neighbor had their bank account levied by the IRS. They put all their money into that account leaving them with no money and little food to eat. They just said to God, "If you are real, help us please." Then here you come knocking on the door with a good word and several bags of groceries. Through your obedience you have now worked with God and His positional pivot system is in operation through you.

We see a case like this in the book of Acts. Saul (who later would become Paul) had a conversion that took the Christian world by surprise to say the least. Ananis in his obedience was positioned right in the middle of it all. Lets read *Acts 9:10-17.*

"And there was a certain disciple at Damascus, named Ananias; and to him said the Lord in a vision, Ananias. And he said, Behold, I am here, Lord. And the Lord said unto him, Arise, and go into the street which is called Straight, and enquire in the house of Judas for one called

Saul, of Tarsus: for, behold, he prays, And hath seen in a vision a man named Ananias coming in, and putting his hand on him, that he might receive his sight. Then Ananias answered, Lord, I have heard by many of this man, how much evil he hath done to thy saints at Jerusalem: And here he hath authority from the chief priests to bind all that call on thy name. But the Lord said unto him, Go thy way: for he is a chosen vessel unto me, to bear my name before the Gentiles, and kings, and the children of Israel: For I will shew him how great things he must suffer for my name's sake. And Ananias went his way, and entered into the house; and putting his hands on him said, Brother Saul, the Lord, even Jesus, that appeared unto thee in the way as thou came, hath sent me, that thou might receive thy sight, and be filled with the Holy Ghost."

We see here that because Ananias was willing to obey, God was able to work through him with his positional pivot system which then lead to Saul's healing and being filled with the Spirit. Positional pivots are riddled throughout the Bible and throughout our lives.

The closest example to this system in the earth would be a gyroscope. If you take a close look at the center of a gyroscope, it always spinning on its original north and south axis causing the whole system to hold its balance. The outer circle is the gyroscope frame, which we can compare to the human body. The inner circle is called the gimbal and we can compare this to the human spirit and soul. The center core is called the rotor, this represents the heart. The rotor spins in one direction, while the gimbal and frame turn another direction. As the gyroscope is spinning, the rotor is keeping the whole structure balanced no matter what is going on with the frame and gimbal.

Another great comparison we have of the gyroscope, is our Heavenly Father, the Son, and the Holy Spirit in relation to the earth. The rotor is sitting between two balancing pins called the spin axis. One of the axis is pointing towards north heaven and the other axis is pointing towards south heaven. We can call the center of this whole moving structure the earth and all its inhabitants. Though the pins are small they carry the greatest importance out of all the mechanized parts because they up hold the rotor in the center. Our Heavenly Father and the Holy Spirit up hold our Lord and His saints along with everything in creation.

Jesus said *John 5:17 "But Jesus answered them, My Father works hitherto, and I work,"* giving the responsibility of super-natural workings to our heavenly Father who was leading and working through Him. In John 14:10 he said, *"Believe thou not that I am in the Father, and the Father in me? The words that I speak unto you I speak not of myself: but the Father that dwells in me, he doeth the works."* Jesus has once again attributed His supernatural behavior to our Heavenly Father.

Romans 8:11 also makes it clear that the Holy Spirit is working to uphold Jesus from a positional pivot point as well. It says "But if the Spirit of him that raised up Jesus from the dead dwell in you, he that raised up Christ from the dead shall also quicken your mortal bodies by his Spirit that dwell in you." This example is a great representation of the three of them working together to keep the complete structure of our being in balance no matter what direction the outer circle, or the people of the world, are going. If Christ is allowed to positionally pivot our lives from the center, the whole structure will continue to stay on point.

Psalms 23:3 says, *"He restores my soul: he leads me in the paths of righteousness for his name's sake.*" Look closely at the colon between the word "soul" and "he leads", you see He opens the statement with the end result. Give me a literary license and I'll show you what I mean. He restores my soul by leading me in paths of righteousness for His Name's sake. You may say, "Wow! You are really taking a chance with that verse." I would agree with you, however, there are just too many examples in the Bible in which we see the positional pivot God is wanting us to be aware of. The most important thing on our end of a positional pivoting is being aware and prepared for God to position as He pleases. Let's look at *Psalms 17:5-9*:

> "*Hold up my goings in thy paths, that my footsteps slip not. I have called upon thee, for thou wilt hear me, O God: incline thine ear unto me, and hear my speech. Shew thy marvellous lovingkindness, you that save by thy right hand them which put their trust in you, from those that rise up against them. Keep me as the apple of the eye, hide me under the shadow of thy wings, from the wicked that oppress me, from my deadly enemies, who compass me about.*"

The key in this passage is the phrase *"Hold my goings in thy paths, that my foot slip not."* Here the Psalmist is aware of God's lovingkindness and confident in the work of his Father's hands by the footprints God left on his life in past situations. He knows God will position him for victory over his enemies; protect him under the shadow of his wings because as he states that God sees him as the apple of His eye. He is aware of the footprints of God's faithfulness to hear him when he calls. Therefore, he has positioned himself for victory! Glory to God!

Another example that shows us God's positional pivoting is *1 Peter 2:24-25*. It states,

> *"Who his own self bare our sins in his own body on the tree, that we, being dead to sins, should live unto righteousness: by whose stripes ye were healed. For ye were as sheep going astray; but are now returned unto the Shepherd and Bishop of your souls."*

Here in these verses the positional pivoting lies in returning to the Shepherd, even when we have gone astray. This is an example of continually being aware of His guiding hand. You cannot return back to the Good Shepherd unless you are aware that you ever left Him to begin with.

No matter where we are in life there is a force that is needed to help keep all Christians balanced properly, this force pulls us back to the center, so that we may be properly positioned. We should have this force ingrained in our every movement in life. The force I'm referring to is the presence of Almighty God, the abundant life Jesus died to give us.

As the earth goes round and round on its axis, so does all the inner workings of God. Each of the four seasons are carefully laid out so that one is never supposed to go before the other. The synergy of grace, pivots from the center of Jesus's heart. Our Heavenly Father designed all things to pivot from the center so that there will always be a balance. It is only when we stray from the center of abiding in Christ Jesus that we cause a great strain on our lives.

This causes fellowshipping with the Father, Son and Holy Spirit next to impossible. As Adam and Eve moved throughout the garden they knew that a great source of energy was located in the center of the garden; the Tree of Life. They ate freely of that tree and that caused their bodies to be rejuvenated with Elohim's life. When God drove them out of the garden His reasoning was to separate them from the Tree of Life so that they could not go back and eat, which, again, caused their bodies to be rejuvenated and death would have its complete and total rein over the human body forever.

We must remember the Lord Jesus Christ originally design the two of them to have complete and total dominion and to reign over all. That was the center of His desire, the positional pivot, if you will, from where He wanted all creation to exist. Jesus was looking to convey a point to the listeners of His day. Let's look at *Luke 17:11-19* and see if we can hook up with Christ here and open our hearts to the message He was conveying.

"And it came to pass, as He (Jesus) went to Jerusalem that he passed through the midst (center) of Samaria and Galilee. And as he entered into a certain village, there met him ten men that were lepers, which stood afar off: and they lifted up their voices, and said, Jesus, Master, have mercy on us. And when he saw them, he said unto them, go shew yourselves unto the priests. And it came to pass, that, as they went, they were cleansed. And one of them, when he saw that he was healed, turned back, and with a loud voice glorified God, and fell down on his face at his feet, giving him thanks: and he was a Samaritan. And Jesus answering said, were there not ten cleansed? But where are the nine? There are not found that returned to give glory to God, save this stranger. And he said unto him, Arise, go thy way: thy faith hath made thee whole."

Jesus was working hard to show his disciples and those who were listening, how to think outside the box of religious hatred of others. Especially the Samarians who were considered outside the positional pivot of God's covenant with Abraham and established through Isaac and Jacob was the foundation of the Jewish nation. However, Samarians considered themselves in perfect positional pivot with God because of their descendants and heritage with the Jewish people. Yet Jesus did not share that view point.

He always speaks from the center. He called the man "a stranger." It is also interesting to note that Jesus knew the Samarians were off pivot. We see this in His statement to the Samarian woman in *John 4:7-13*

"There came a woman of Samaria to draw water: Jesus said to her, Give me to drink. (For his disciples were gone away unto the city to buy meat.) Then said the woman of Samaria unto him, how is it that you, being a Jew, ask drink of me, which am a woman of Samaria?"

Now drop down to verses 20-23.

"Our fathers worshipped in this mountain; and ye say, that in Jerusalem is the place where men ought to worship. Jesus said unto her, Woman, believe me, the hour comes, when you shall neither in this mountain, nor yet at Jerusalem, worship the Father. You worship what you know not of: we know what we worship: for salvation is of the Jews. But the hour comes, and now is, when the true worshippers shall worship the Father in spirit and in truth: for the Father seeks such to worship him."

Jesus was clear concerning their misconception of Who His Father was. *"You worship what you know not of."* I believe the Samaritan man took Jesus by surprise when he actually knew to whom he was worshiping and positioned his heart in humility to receive the mighty grace our Heavenly Father was offering toward him. The power of the Holy Spirit and Jesus Christ changed the lives of the leprous man and the woman at well forever.

When Jesus recognized the positional pivot in their lives, He made a point of showing those who were looking on that faith in God belongs to every person. He wanted to prove to them that our Heavenly Father is very liberal in distributing his healing to all who will have faith in the Son of God.

I used the word "positional pivot" so you would understand how the spiritual and mental side of the heart were working together to line this man and woman up so God's overwhelming grace might work for them.

First of all, God the Father put Jesus in the center of this town. Jesus passed through the middle of Samaria and Galilee; this was a leading not a coincidence. Secondly, the leprous man cried out with a loud voice and called Him Master and looked to Him, as someone who, through His mercy, could make a difference in his life.

Notice how he was willing to speak what he was processing in his heart. Jesus also gave him the proper procedure under the Law of Moses for those who were healed of this type of disease. So, in other words, he spoke and acted on the positional pivot that was presented or directing him in his heart. Jesus positioned him towards the Law; however, something short-circuited the process in this man's heart. He knew what Jesus told him but thanksgiving overwhelmed him in such a way he had to go worship the champion of his faith. It is good to remember when you are confronted with God's procedural law (which He implemented through Moses) it will always give way to His LOVE unleashed, which passes knowledge. Our Heavenly Father is desiring all people to have this unleashed form of LOVE. That is what the Samarian man tapped into. In great humility he fell down at his feet in total surrender to any form of pride. I can imagine God in heaven and all the heavenly host watching that high praise and worship; the same worship Jesus gave reference to when He was speaking to the Samaritan woman at the well. Jesus said, "Give glory to God."

It is the same with us when our positional pivot of praise and worship to Our Heavenly Father is lifted up and we are reflecting on His goodness towards us. When we do this, help will always come. Jesus promised. Remember, beloved of God, the battle for the positional pivot in our live is two types of thought and only two! Who will we surrender control of our heart to and why surrender to that entity?

You see the other nine were healed, but they did not surrender to the spiritual force of thanksgiving that would have pivoted their healing into worship that would have cleansed their soul. You see when God's power is used to heal your body and your soul is not cleaned often time you find yourself back in the same poor physical condition once again. The nine only gave Yeshua access to their need and denied Him access to cause of their need. Nine refused to yield to the call of the Spirit and come to the center.

You might wonder why I said that, but if you look at verse thirteen you can see they were positioned in the center of God's pivot system for their lives. He brought Jesus by them for that very reason and, even though they seized the opportunity, they did not seize their destiny.

When healing came, why didn't they reposition their hearts to do something else like offer thanksgiving like the Samaritan man? Well, I'm glad you asked. The truth is people are doing it all over the world. Sadly, many are not getting their healing, or are losing it completely after they got it, because of their lack of worship through thanksgiving to the Father. As I said before, the heart only processes what you allow into it and the Spirit knows the exact positional pivot required to receive and to keep anything given from God.

I would like to point something else out to you. Of the ten lepers, nine of them were Jews. We know this to be true because Jesus would not have told them to do what the Law of Moses expected of them. If they were outsiders they would not have understood him. How can we know this about the Samaritan? Well, they were accustom to the Law of Moses because they considered themselves part of the Abrahamic covenant. Ancestrally, Samaritans "claim" they were the descendants from the Israelite tribes of Ephraim and Manasseh (two sons of Joseph) as well as from the priestly tribe of Levi. Remember what the woman at well said, "...our father Jacob"— implying a covenant through Abraham.

Look with me at what Jesus prescribed for the ten lepers. He said, "Go show yourselves to the priest." This is exactly what God told Moses to have His people do when they were healed of this terrible disease. Jesus knew the Jews and Samaritans understood what He meant when He told them to do that.

One might argue, "Yes but Jesus said 'go.'" My reply to that is they could have yielded to the Spirit, went back and offered up thanksgiving from a seat of worship, and then went and showed themselves to the priest. Of course this makes no sense to the religious mental portion of the heart. When religion leads someone, they will always stick to the letter of the law.

Here is an example of what I mean. Say God heals a person simply because He wants to out of His mercy and grace. Then that person attributes their God given healing, to their own good works. They begin to scoff at people who, in their estimation, don't deserve God's goodness because of their lifestyle. However, in their religious minds they never connect the dots enough to understand that their healing is only a pure act of God's grace and compassion on their lives.

Then satan spins his little web of seduction, tying them all up in knots and taking their healing from the center of their soul. We find it spelled out clearly in *Matthew 6:1-34* Jesus starts His teaching with a pivotal alignment by guiding them into the proper way to give to the poor. He then begins to give us more clarity on how to pray. Jesus reveals to us the pivot point from which all covenant people must make their stand. He begins by stating, *"No man can serve two masters"* (or no rotor can pivot on two centers). This mammon thought process is God's archenemy.

Just like the rotor of the gyroscope continually pivot on its axis, our axis must continually have Christ in the center in order for us to properly benefit from all He died and now lives for. If the gyroscope of life is knocked off its axis at any time it will cease to keep balance and we find ourselves in defeat of God's mature purpose for our lives as believers. So rather than filling your heart with worry, fear and self-reliance, which is the mammon way, search for Christ's way of doing and living in the Kingdom.

Consequently, the laws of His grace that will see to our supply. Each one of these Kingdom statements from verses 1 - 21 are positional pivot statements for all Christians. They are milk for the mature believer, however, they know the Mighty Teacher has given them real meat to live by as well. *Matthew 6:22-34* says,

"The light of the body is the eye: if therefore thine eye be single, thy whole body shall be full of light. But if thine eye be evil, thy whole body shall be full of darkness. If therefore the light that is in thee be darkness, how great is that darkness! No man can serve two masters: for either he will hate the one, and love the other; or else he will hold to the one, and despise the other. You cannot serve God and mammon. Therefore I say unto you, Take no thought for your life, what ye shall eat, or what ye shall drink; nor yet for your body, what you will put on. Is not the life more than meat, and the body than raiment? Behold the fowls of the air: for they sow not, neither do they reap, nor gather into barns; yet your heavenly Father feeds them. Are ye not much better than they? Which of you by taking thought can add one cubit unto his stature? And why take you thought for raiment? Consider the lilies of the field, how they grow; they toil not, neither do they spin: and yet I say unto you, that even Solomon in all his glory was not arrayed like one of these. Wherefore, if God so clothe the grass of the field, which today is, and tomorrow is cast into the oven, shall he not much more clothe you. You of little faith? Therefore take no thought, saying, what shall we eat? Or what shall we drink? Or, wherewith will we be clothed? For after all these things do the Gentiles seek: for your heavenly Father knows that you have need of all these things. But seek you first the kingdom of God, and his righteousness; and all these things shall be added unto you. Take therefore no thought for the morrow: for the morrow shall take thought for the things of itself. Sufficient unto the day is the evil thereof."

We can find the positional pivot in verse 22. Jesus is referring to how the heart processes the issues of life by saying *"the light of the body is the eye."* You could say it as the gathering of information in the spirit and soul portion of your heart (which dwell in your body) is the eye. Then He goes on to say, *"if therefore your eye be single, your whole body shall be full of light."* So, if your eye processes the Word of His Spirit the way He trained it to, the two dimensions in a person will be illuminated in the body.

The procedure works the same in the darkest place in the processor, but there is a difference. Notice Jesus put heavy emphasis on the darkness over the light. It is because the spirit and soul of all people were dead to God. However, under the new covenant, in a believer's life the processing mechanism has a great advantage. Not only is the light being processed through the eye but it is hooking up with the light manufacturer inside us. It has the capability of flooding the dead soul or mind with our Father's positional pivot for each thought and act of the day.

Positional pivoting is His way of guiding us through life thoughts so that when our enemy, Death and his side-kick, Condemnation, begin pressing us we must remember that we are to live from the center. Jesus is encouraging us to, as He put it, *"take no thought for your life."* Why? Because He will give you the right thought to process so your whole body can successfully be empowered to overcome these crafty enemies.

Jesus is spelling out a Kingdom-of-God-way-of-living verses the kingdom-of-man-way-of-living. It is interesting that six times He brings up "thought" as the darkness His people should not be living for and six just happens to be the number for man. The carnal six are the self-sufficiency Death and Condemnation survive off of.

The thought He wants us to have is of the mercy and grace

that carries all things from the center and pours out on us in abundance. We need to put His thoughts in our processor and produce the faith it take to receive it.

One time my wife and I were dealing with a very hard-pressed financial situation. We had rental properties and our yearly taxes were due on all of our properties on a certain date. We had a house in escrow closing before that date; however, the person backed out of the deal the day before they were supposed to sign the papers on the house.

I remember standing in the living room with my head hanging low. I felt like someone had punched me right in the gut. I was so defeated I could not even raise my hands to worship God, which is what we usually do in the mornings. Suddenly I heard the voice of the Lord say, "If you don't faint I will not let you fail." When our Lord said that it filled me full of light and I changed my thoughts to His thoughts and I said in my heart, "I don't have all these thousands of dollars to give the tax people, but I do know how to have my faith for the money." So I said, "Heavenly Father, I'm asking you for the money to pay my taxes." Then I began to mediate on *Matthew 17:24-27.*

> "*When they were come to Capernaum, they that received tribute money came to Peter, and said, Doth not your master pay tribute? He said, yes. And when he was come into the house, Jesus prevented him, saying, what do you think, Simon? Of whom do the kings of the earth take custom or tribute? of their own children, or of strangers? Peter said to him, "of strangers". Jesus said unto him, then are the children free. Notwithstanding, lest we should offend them, go thou to the sea, and cast an hook, and take up the fish that first cometh up; and*

when thou hast opened his mouth, thou shalt find a piece of money: that take, and give unto them for me and thee."

I know Jesus had set a positional pivot for my tax money. All I had to do was think from the center and I did just that. The money came in right before tax day and we were free from the unrighteous mammon pressing us.

Chapter 5
Positional Origin

"In the beginning God created the heavens and earth."
Genesis 1:1

This statement gives us clarity as to who designed the "positional origin" of creation. God is a Spirit; therefore, we know the inner workings of creation are not only physical but spiritual as well.

What is a positional origin? A positional origin is the axis in which all creation was placed. This axis has seven dimensions operating simultaneously. In the Book of Origins (Genesis) we find positional origin in operation with the restoration of the plant. I will show you what I mean.

John Chapter 1 opens the door to the mystery behind the why and the how of creation. It states,

"In the beginning was the Word and the Word was with God and the Word was God the same was in the beginning with God all things were made by him and without him was not anything made that was made in Him was life and the light of man." John 1:1-4

You see saints of God, we received our origin from life and the light of our origin was solely for the purpose of the light: Jesus Christ. We find Him referenced here in *Colossians 1:15-17,*

> *"Who is the image of the invisible creator the first-born of every creature for by him were all things created that are in heaven and that are in earth visible and invisible whether they be Thrones or dominions principalities or power all things were created by him and for him and he is before all things and by him all things exist."*

People have searched for hundreds and hundreds of years for the origin in order to position themselves properly. However, we know that the living and true origin only exist in the Creator's plan and dreams for humans. These plans have spanned the globe for thousands of years. We see it documented among the faithful listed in the book of Hebrews. These documentations are accurate positional origins of faith in the world we know today.

> *"Through faith we understand that the worlds were framed by the word of God so that things which are seen were not made of things which do appear." Hebrews 11:3*

The word "world" literally means "ages." So another translation of that first statement would be, "we understand that the 'ages' were affected by the Word of God" through faith. I like to think that the ages were brought back into positional origin by faith in the Word of God. The effect God wanted to have in keeping the "age" would only be the effect He originally intended and not affect the people of that age. Here is what I mean. God gave the Jewish people the promise land, however there were others in that land using it for their own intensions. God told the Jewish people to remove them and He had every right because the land belongs to the Creator. *Psalms 47:7* and *8 For God is King of all the earth: sing ye praises with understanding. God reign over the heathen: God sit upon the throne of His holiness.*

So as you read Chapter 11 it is giving clarity to each person's grace in helping God bring all things back to their positional origin. Abraham, Isaac, and Jacob (Israel) had a great effect on their "age"/environment. No man successfully stood in their way as long as they acted with clarity concerning the Creator's positional origin. They also did not consider each circumstance that was before them.

They all made their mistakes such as with Hagar, which was never God's desire for Abraham and Sarah's positional origin. Laban was never God's desire for Jacob's positional origin. However, when presented with the positional origin of what He desired they surrendered their lives and affected the world/ages around them by faith.

Nothing has changed concerning our Heavenly Father's thinking in this matter. He gave us His Word, our Lord Jesus Christ, to affect the age we live in now from the center of His good will. In the center He hides His plan, purposes, and pursuits for His people. Why else would He bring a people about out of the loins of other people who were not a special (chosen) people to Him?

When you search the chronicles you look down through the ages our Heavenly Father had a special relationship with individuals, but His desire was a nation or a group of people to reveal Himself through and to the rest of the people on earth. There was nothing special about these people without Him. Nevertheless, the positional origin was placed on them from the foundation of the world.

God searched for the right couple who would fit the bill, as we say. It's interesting that we always say Abraham was chosen because he would teach his children, but Sarah played a key role in teaching young Isaac and even more so because she would carry him for nine months.

God has given women an awesome responsibility to carry His most prized possession and it is a great honor for them. A woman has the unique ability of receiving a seed from her husband at a certain season. When that seed is placed in the positional origin in the proper environment for his seed and her egg to meet, conception takes place as the divine distribution of light (spirit and soul) which causes the body to group, the spirit, and soul are placed in the body.

One might wonder how does the spirit and soul know when to come to the earth? How does it get here? When two people come together and engage in the baby-making procedure, their souls are being tied as one soul and body, and their spirits are sending positional origin signals to our Heavenly Father's throne, the angels witness this act and watch with great excitement awaiting the call from the Heavenly Father to come get one of those souls. Most signals are very weak because doing the procedure is common and frequent,(and most of the times with great pleasure I might add). When the male instrument enters the female gate it boils over with excitement to go deeper and the keeper of the gate (is located above the gate entrance) is crying out for more width and depth. God is okay with the whole procedure, because the positional origin of it all is from Him. He considers it beautiful. The Lord could have chosen a million different ways to complete His baby making procedure but chose this one. His purpose is much more important than the procedure even though we enjoy it.

However, there is a much greater plan while all this is going on. Creation is being performed because the hidden elements are yet to come into play and complete soul ties are connected irruption takes place. That's why His Word puts great emphasis on staying away from adultery and fornication.

There are two reasons. The first one is the soul tie aspect, which is very real and quite potent. The issues of life that are in the soul portion of your heart are connecting with the soul portion of the heart of the other person. If their body is full of darkness, that darkness is poured right into you. This is why most prostitutes, male and female, use drugs. They think they can rid themselves of the darkness. However, they cannot because the "cleaving process" was design for positional origin purposes.

Almighty God put the "cleaving process" in place when a husband and wife becomes one flesh. Their souls are connecting and communicating with one another in harmonious balance the way God intended it to be in the beginning. This is how a mother's training for her baby begins while the child is still in her body. The second reason God hates adultery and fornication is better explained like this.

Imagine, if you can, when conception is taking place that little baby is sown in a physically protected environment, but when the act of adultery and fornication takes place during conception, the baby feels the guilt and shame or whatever the heart is full of immediately because it is forming right next to the core of the heart in the mother's belly. Remember what Jesus said in *John 7:38-39*.

"He that believes on me, as the scripture hath said, out of his belly shall flow rivers of living water. (But this

spoke he of the Spirit, which they that believe on him should receive: for the Holy Ghost was not yet given; because that Jesus was not yet glorified.)

We know God the Father, God the Son, and God the Holy Spirit dwell in the spirit portion of our heart. Our Heavenly Father is very much aware of the immortal acts. I would say more than any other act that people will do outside of accepting Jesus as their Lord and Savior. God the Father is Lord of the Harvest and it gives Him great pleasure to send His prize possessions down here. Each spirit/soul/body creation has in it a positional origin that is called to be fulfilled. Christ opened a new and living way for His precious creation, the first and most important call is to accept Him. However, it becomes very strong when conception occurs. He then sends an angel faster than you can blink an eye with a new spirit and soul and places it in the center of that human body. Then that angel records every stage of that child's development throughout its life here on earth. You may say that is too juvenile. No, it's the simplicity of positional origin. Remember Adam's spirit and soul was placed in his body by God in the beginning.

Let us look at the Scripture for more clarity, Jesus gives us a glimpse in *Matthew 18:10:*

> *"Take heed that you despise not one of these little ones; for I say unto you, that in heaven their angels do always behold the face of my Father which is in heaven."*

Notice Jesus said "their" angels. The word "their" denotes possession or ownership. These awesome beings are with all humans while we are here on earth, helping and recording our every move. Now I said they bring the life of God down and places it in the body. You might wonder what body? There is just a seed and egg! Yes, you are right. However, because you lack knowledge of the procedure, you are thinking naturally like a carnal scientist. You think the body is a body when it is fully developed, and what medical science calls a "fetus," but God created the body and at conception it is very small at first and begins to grow. In His eyes there is no such thing as an unformed body. He considers it as a growing person's body. You would not look at a girl who is five years old and say she is unformed would you? No, she is a growing person and developing into a beautiful women. It's the same thing in His eyes. Let's look some more at this process in *Luke 1:35*

> *"And the angel answered and said unto her, The Holy Ghost shall come upon thee, and the power of the Highest shall overshadow thee: therefore also that holy thing which shall be born of thee shall be called the Son of God."*

NOW PLEASE turn off your religious minds for a second and remember the angel is talking about plan/purpose and procedure. I find it apropos that an angel was used of God to explain this overshadowing procedure to Mary because it was so different from what they knew. In the case of Jesus, the Holy Spirit did the honor of the procedure. The Holy Spirit did for Jesus what our angel does for us. (When they come upon our parents and breathed life in our little bodies.) That is He implanted Jesus's spirit and soul in His body to bring the body to life and record. Jesus' every move was to help Him fulfill our Heavenly Father's complete positional origin in Jesus' life *1 John 5:5-6*

"This is he that came by water and blood, even Jesus Christ; not by water only, but by water and blood. And it is the Spirit that bear witness, because the Spirit is truth. For there are three that bear record in heaven, the Father, the Word, and the Holy Ghost: and these three are one. And there are three that bear witness in earth, the Spirit, and the water, and the blood: and these three agree in one." 1 John 5:6-8

He was positioned to be sown in death and resurrection in life. Oftentimes the credit for things designed or invented on the earth is given to people. However, what we are really looking at is our Heavenly Father's desire either carried out through His children or by the carnal world. The reason why we are confused as to its origin is because He uses the world to design or invent it and not His children, even though His children are His first choice. Only a believer can know the positional origin of a thing with accuracy when they have everything lined in the center through the Word of God and the leading of the Spirit. When that happens, then we see His original intent.

An example of this positional origin is when Nimrod and his followers decided to build a city and a tower. God had no problem with that, but He did have a problem with them making a name for themselves because His positional origin was that there would be one name under heaven for all people in the earth; the Name of Jesus. Let's look at this destructive thought.

"And they said, Go to, let us build us a city and a tower, whose top may reach unto heaven; and let us make us a name, lest we be scattered abroad upon the face of the whole earth. And the LORD came down to see the city and

the tower, which the children of men built." Genesis 11:4-5

This thought of self-reliance did not fit inside the statement Jesus made in Matthew 6 when He said *"on earth as it is in heaven."* There was no plan for people to make a name for themselves in God's plan in heaven. You see these people had no intention of serving the living Creator. They were building towers and such to worship themselves. That's why He takes you and I and places us in the center of a matter. Then He begins to tell us what His will is.

You and I have heard testimonies from different people who changed the purpose of a strip mall, a commercial building, a stadium, electronic device, and satellites media from the original intent back to God's positional origin when He sent the idea down here in the first place. Mark my words, there shall soon arise a social media for believers only and the list goes on. It is our Lord Jesus Christ bringing all things to the center so that the positional origin is once again pure and undefiled. Remember all things were made by Him and for Him.

Let me also say to the moms out there, your unborn baby has come from the presence of Almighty God and has been there enjoying the wonders of His love. While I know you can't duplicate that environment, you can fill your house with praise and worship, which causes just the right atmosphere for your beautiful baby to grow with God's love in their heart. Remember, your baby is located very close to your spiritual heart. You must be extremely careful about keeping your conscience clear of offense along with other demonstrative acts and thoughts. Take time to sow good thought from the Word of God and good verbal communication as much as you can.

To give you an idea how important it is, it reminds me of

a man who had a daughter-in-law that could not stand him. She had what we call "daddy issues" and she also had a real problem with authority. On top of that, he was a very take charge person (as we say) so when she was pregnant and was around him, even though she could not stand him, she would put on like she cared for him like our people that loved him did. However, what she did not know was that she was training her unborn baby to dislike him. When the child was introduced to him, it let the cat out of the bag. The baby would immediately cry and push away even as infants can often do. Her secret was out he said. All of her children did the same thing until they got to be four or five years old. By then they would see what a loving person he was and they loved him.

Now don't get me wrong. I'm not saying this is true in all cases where a baby does not take to a person; however, I do find the correlation interesting. The man went on to say his other daughter-in-law loved him and his wife deeply. Her children would run up to him with open arms and loving smiles. Truthfully, all that the first daughter-in-law had to do was yield to the positional origin of God's love from the center of her heart, and begin to use His Word to cast down those vain imaginations bringing them into the obedience of Christ's networking system and her soul would have been cleansed of all her daddy issues. Then God our Father would have met her with an overwhelming amount of deliverance for her and her children.

I shared some of these truths with my prayer and Bible Study group one day. A dear sister spoke up and said, "That's very interesting. When I had my first daughter, I craved in my heart chocolate and vanilla ice cream and to this day my daughter craves the same. But with my second daughter my craving was different and she craves the other foods. It is important to remember moms your order of business is LOVE and then all people will Love our Lord of Glory.

Prophetic Utterance

Great unbelief will fill the earth like a plague. Run, little children. Run to the threshing floor like King David did, and purchase the floor with your praise, offer up a sacrifice worthy of honor to Me, even a sacrifice of pure worship; that the great plague will stop and the people may know the "justified ones shall live by faith". Then all peoples in the earth will see My glory. Says The Lord of Host!

Chapter 6

Spirit, Soul and Body

The heart is God's fascinating creation and it has a sense of unity in one important aspect. Each of the three divided portions (spirit, soul and body) have a chamber located in it. Now when I say "body," I am not talking about our physical body being in the spiritual heart. I am, however, talking about our physical body sending signals to the heart.

You can test this statement when you pay close attention to your body when it smells a food you really like. Watch it send a signal to your heart through your mind. That's how flesh sins get in the heart. A man or a woman's body is aroused by a person's cologne before they see the person, and tells their soul, "I want that." If something that attracts you is at the end of that fragrance, your spirit, soul and body will have temptation to deal with, like it or not!

"For the word of God is quick, and powerful, and sharper than any two edged sword, piercing even to the dividing asunder of soul and spirit, and of the joints and marrow, and is a discerner of the thoughts and intents of the heart." Hebrews 4:12

It show us here how God's Word can see into us with pin point accuracy and not miss a beat in locating where we are in our spiritual walk with Him at all times. It enters this centrally located processor and speaks to all three when necessary. It is always searching for new ways of expressing itself. The spirit is directly connected to God. Proverbs puts it this way:

> *"The spirit of a person is the candle of the LORD, searching all the inward parts of the belly." Proverbs 20:27*

Our spirit handles the light of God because it is light. You may wonder in this case what is searching for in the belly or dwelling place of the heart. It's searching for righteousness, truth, justice or the righteous way so that it may lead the soul and body portion of the heart. Our spirit has the amazing ability to yield to God's Word in our daily affairs. In other cases it searches for answers to help us in our daily affairs. Now we must remember that our soul is dead, but it is still a magnificent creation. It has the ability to send signals to the soulish portion of the heart as they are received from the center. Then the soul begins to put in motion what it has received from the spiritual realm, or natural realm, and depending on what information it is given, will be the actions you will see.

I like what I heard a man say once concerning our tripartite being. He said we are spirit; we have a soul; and we live in a body. I find it difficult to improve on that description of human beings so we will stay with that.

When God created man it was His desire to fellowship with Him on three planes: spirit, soul and body. Each of these have their own unique place in our Heavenly Father's heart. That's why Jesus died for us. He died for the whole person. When He created Adam, a living soul His greatest fellowship with him was mainly in the soulish realm.

*"And so it is written, The first man Adam was made
a living soul;" 1 Corinthians 15:45*

What is a living soul? It is a soul that has light/life in it,
meaning from the core of its origin is light and there is no
darkness at all. God's Word said this in *John 1: 4*

"In him (Jesus) was life; and the life was the light of man."

When Adam and Eve ate the fruit that was forbidden,
they died. In other words, the light became dark in their soul
and spirit. They became aliens to the living light according to
Colossians 1:21.

*"And you, that were sometime alienated and enemies
in your mind by wicked works, yet now hath he reconciled."*

It is interesting to note that the enemy of God is a dead
soul or a dead mind. Why an enemy? Because God designed
his light to dwell in the center so that all humans may fellowship with Him from the center. However, with this new dead
mind the center has been compromised and twisted works
are the only thing it can produce.

The Word of God can no longer guide man with accuracy
without the light present. Through Christ Jesus, He created
a new person who is a quickening spirit according to *1 Corinthians 15:45, "the last Adam was made a quickening spirit."*
So the Lord Jesus Christ can now fellowship and guide his
people from the center. However, it doesn't end there. He still
has the difficult task of dealing with our dead soul. That's why
we are encouraged to renew our mind/soul.

"And be not conformed to this world: but be ye trans-formed by the renewing of your mind, that ye may prove what is that good, and acceptable, and perfect, will of God." Romans 12:2

Just as a side thought, when you search the word concerning the soul in Hebrew, it spells out the soul of an animal applying it to people. Adam and Eve were given portions of the same mental DNA as animals. So with this living soul they could fellowshipped in unity and communicated with all creation including the animals.

We know this is true because Eve did not freak out when the serpent spoke to her. If they couldn't talk with the animals, I imagine her first question to the serpent would have been, "How are you able to speak to me?" We lost the ability to communicate with animals when confusion fell on all creation through the death of our spirit and soul. However, in heaven animals speak. If you don't think so then go read the *Book of Revelation 6:1*

"And I saw when the Lamb opened one of the seals, and I heard, as it were the noise of thunder, one of the four beasts saying."

Yes, the souls of humans and animals were made compatible in order for there to be harmony in the garden. Adam and Eve had light/life in their soul but their spirit was dormant, having only a small flicker of light as it were. Their reasoning capacity was only centered on the five physical senses, which makes up the foundation of the soul but very little spiritual illumination. Christ encourages us to renew our mind so that His Word will dominate the five physical senses and work with our quickening spirit.

I said the "spirit was dormant" and only had a flicker of light because God had fully intended to dwell in the spirit of humans. He allowed His creation to be subject to death; spirit soul and body. A limited soul was no comparison to a limitless spirit. If you were to compare the two, the spirit is enormous in comparison.

We see a glimpse of this in *Mark 5:3-9* when the evil spirit reply to Jesus' question, *"What is your name?" He said, "My name is legion for we are many."* A legion in the Roman armed forces was approximately one to five thousand soldiers. These unclean spirits in this case were numbered at two thousand. Can you imagine two thousand evil spirits inside a human spirit? That gives you some idea of how enormous the human spirit of a person is. God knew the spirit had to carry such vast space because He was going to dwell in it Himself. Can you fathom the depth of God dwelling in the human spirit?

There are great depictions in the world of many things, however this depiction carries the "tilt factor." Our spirit was regenerated to house the Word of God, the Spirit of God, and God the Father. God would like to fellowship with you Spirit to spirit. The difficulty comes when we decide to walk in the flesh or live as though we are dead when Christ paid the ultimate sacrifice so that we might live like quickening spirits.

Death and life dwell in us, however, we can control death by making a lifestyle of living in the light. Training our soul is His mandate to us. The soul will do exactly what any good computer will do. If you put light or living information in it, the Word of God will then begin to communicate with the light thereby causing death to be influenced by the light. I call it the light factor. The more light you put in the soul/mind the more it will gravitate towards our Heavenly Father's will for our lives and the lives we touch.

I do not want to minimize the power of the human soul because Adam named all the animals, bugs, birds and fish. His capacity to assimilate and process what God put before him is hard to fathom. Adam and Eve thought and comprehended with lightning fast speed. The two of them were super intelligent beings. Their bodies were so full of energy and light that they enjoyed abnormal strength. All they have to do to keep strength, was eat the living foods in the garden and eat from the tree of life. I have to admit that was one of the most disappointing parts of the fall; having our bodies subjected to death. Even though that's all we know, they were different. They knew a time with no death. I look forward to the day when it becomes a reality that our new bodies will walk on air without submitting to the elements of the earth.

"In a moment, in the twinkling of an eye, at the last trump: for the trumpet shall sound, and the dead shall be raised incorruptible, and we shall be changed."
1 Corinthians 15:52

"And the armies which were in heaven followed him (in the air) upon white horses, clothed in fine linen, white and clean." Revelation 19:14

Now when God designs anything it is always from the center. I'm amused when I hear secular scientists speak of God's ecosystems. They speak of creation after it is created. Therefore, they are discovering the origin, not implementing or designing through creative genius, of any kind. Just plain old boring discovery.

When we look closely His purpose concerning the ecosystems we find out He designed the ecosystems because he wanted it that way. Not because it had any other purpose than His desire. It is important to understand how I mean that, which leads to another tilt factor. He designed trees to be green because He likes green and built an ecosystem around it. If He wanted the trees to be red, He would have built an ecosystem around red trees. The church of God must be careful it does not fall into the same foolish thinking as secular science by making Christ fit their little mold thereby causing human stumbling blocks of grace-filled traditions and faithless living before the world. All things were made by Him and without Him there was not anything made that was made. We must always remember science is a by-product that follows the Creator, especially when it comes to divinely-inspired intelligent design.

Prophetic Order

"How shall I compare this generation (speaking of the Jews)? It is like children sitting in the market and calling on to their fellows and saying we have piped unto you and you have not danced, we have mourned unto you and you have not lamented" Matthew 11:16-17

Jesus was very clear concerning His assessment of the Jewish people. They were so far from the center that in their spoiled and confused state they could not come to believe and see the goodness of the Lord in the land of the living. Now Christ is looking at the Church and He says,

"How shall I compare this generation? I have brought you great miracles. You have learn more about Me than any other time on the earth. I have manifested my presents through my Spirit in marvelous ways and you are like the world. You want to sing and dance and play. You want Me to mourn over your dead when you yourselves are like clouds without rain, children, confused and so far from the center of My purpose for you that your confusion is spewed out on the world and is drawing them further away from Me. You want to blow your instruments of worldly pleasure and call on Me to sing and dance. As you mourn for your dead, you call on Me to comfort you.

"I'm calling you now to take your place as kings of purpose. Not as those who are under condemnation, but as ones resurrected in a mighty and vast Kingdom. Shake off those grave clothes and I will give you the proper ropes of life that will be needed for this final harvest of souls. I personally made them for you, as Jacob did for Joseph when he made him the robe of many colors. Then you will carry yourselves like children of kindness and goodness the same way that you have received from Me all these many years, and you shall be called "Instruments of Reaping" in this last harvest of souls.

"I, the LORD, have spoken and will not repent. To those of my children that have an ear to hear, let them hear what the Spirit of the Lord is saying. All those who take their part in this final harvest of souls will be kings of purpose and no man shall stand before you all the days of your life. I shall make my pillar of grace amongst your children and amongst their children as an offering of thanksgiving for your obedience to My Spirit.

"Amen and Amen."

Chapter 7
Father, Son, Holy Spirit

"Behold I will send you Elijah the prophet before the coming of the Great and dreadful day of the Lord: and He shall turn the heart of the fathers to the children and the heart of the children to their fathers."

In part of this passage we see our Heavenly Father has put a premium on the fathers taking their center place and the children reciprocating. I know that all things that pertain to life and godliness in a proper family environment has to evolve from the center of God the Father, God the Son, God the Holy Spirit. In *John 3:16* it says for *"God so loved the people of the world that He gave."* Giving is a necessary ingredient to a father not only guiding his household from the center, but God also expects us to yield to one another's gifting and calling that He has given us. Our Heavenly Father believes very deeply in unity. So deeply so that He cautions married believers not to hinder their prayers by walking in disunity and dishonor toward one another.

"Likewise, husbands, dwell with them (your own wife) according to knowledge, giving honor unto the wife, as unto the weaker vessel, and as being heirs together of the grace of life; that your prayers be not hindered." 1 Peter 3:7

Let me also say that when the Spirit of God says through Apostle Paul *"live with her according to knowledge"* He speaks of spiritual knowledge, but let us not set aside earthly knowledge as well.

To give you an example, when my wife and I were first married in the 80's. We were young and I was dwelling with her from a newlywed's perspective. However, after I had ten years, three kids, a car payment, a house payment, both of us finished with school and had our careers well on the way, I was dwelling with her under a far different parameters of knowledge. After having twenty years under my belt, the dwelling with her according to knowledge scenario changed again. The same occurred after thirty years, five kids, two daughters-in-law, one son-in-law, five grandkids, three businesses and all the ministry affairs etc. (the learning curve I must say is one for the books).

Nevertheless, with each season comes a paradigm shift. It also brought great comfort to know The Lord was and is there helping and teaching me how to dwell with her according to knowledge. The funny part is He is so subtle in His help at times, I sometimes did not know it was Him helping me.

I remember one summer morning I was sitting in my Tuesday prayer and Bible Study group, gazing out the window at the lake and just enjoying the beautiful scenery. Then one the ladies commented on how romantic Jesus was. That statement immediately got my attention and I thought, "She's wrong." I've never known Jesus to be romantic and then the Lord Jesus spoke up in my heart. He said, "Oh yeah? Where do you think you've been getting all those romantic ideas you've been using on your wife all these years?" "Oh," I said sheepishly. "That's right!"

A wise man once said "Love is the shoulders honor stands on while peeking over the wall of human relationships, beckoning all to climb the wall and enjoy its goods" I find those words to be so true. Jesus describes dishonor and disunity as a walled in place where so many find themselves because they refuse to live from the center. These two evil characters, dishonor and disunity, feel they have a right to every human relationship born into their domain. To allow Adam's people to climb over wall and walk in the plan of God is absurd to them. So Our Heavenly Father through the plan of redemption bought us out of this oppressing dishonorable behavior and had very somber thoughts as to how He would deal with it in the future of humanity.

> *"And the LORD smelled a sweet savour; and the LORD said in his heart, I will not again curse the ground any more for man's sake; for the imagination of man's heart is evil from his youth; neither will I again smite any more everything living, as I have done." Genesis 8:21*

God hates disunity and dishonor, however, He wants to save His people, which is a delicate surgery. He has to reach inside of a human's encapsulated heart (which I might add was completely sealed in darkness) and make a circumcision in it. Then restore (completely walled in) a place for Him to live. The Bible calls it circumcision of the heart.

> *"But he is a Jew, which is one inwardly; and circumcision is that of the heart, in the spirit, and not in the letter; whose praise is not of men, but of God." Romans 2:29*

It is important to reiterate that our Heavenly Father takes His Word and the blood of Jesus through the witness and power of the Holy Spirit to do the surgery Himself. He gave us a clue as to why this is!

Notice this statement "Lord said in His heart." When we look at the statement "in His heart," we understand "in His heart" is the origin and the pivoting point of all that is good and pure and proper for humanity. The Lord Himself has all things that pertain to life and godliness pivoting from the center of His heart. The Words in Scripture mentioned above are carefully chosen by Him out of love and mercy for humanity. He knows the evil that is in a person's heart after the fall of Adam and Eve. He knows it is not going to be removed by a strong hand of judgement, yet, as we watch Him from Genesis to Revelation, He gently works His plan to remove this evil from our hearts. He calls it love for humanity. It brought Him to the place of complete and total divine sacrifice.

You may find it strange that I said" He calls it love" but that is the only way to describe who He is and what He does. The divine definition of LOVE is to pour out your life for the undesiring with no guarantee of compensation for your deed. You see, only He can name the origin of a matter from the center, and the center is LOVE. To recognize the origin of what He is doing is purely an act of His mercy. Otherwise we would never discover the center of His thinking. The Scripture refers to this process as being blind.

For example the center point of our salvation was when our heavenly Father formed a people in the earth through Abraham and Sarah, He created the perfect environment (the Jewish nation) for His Son to be sown into. Those from the outside (the foolish religious people among the Jews) were very hostile toward Him because they were blind to His purpose.

We have learned as farmers to always sow seed in the center. You may say, "What center? Are you saying "the center of the earth?" No! The seed receives its center directly in the origin of its growth. Meaning where ever you sow it, if the soil is good, that is the center. God programed a husband to give his wife his seed in the center. It is the most fertile place a seed can be sown to produce, it is the hiding place. So by sowing His love in the center of people's heart through salvation, it has allowed us to be in connection with His divine nature as His children. All people who have this nature sewn in them can communicate from the center without disunity or dishonor through shame.

Now the way He views this new nature and the good He has placed in us is clearly spelled out in *Matthew 7:17-18.*

> *Even so every good tree brings forth good fruit but a corrupt tree brings forth evil fruit a good tree cannot bring forth evil fruit neither can a corrupt tree bring forth good fruit.*

Jesus was chosen from the center of God's plan. When you look at the full plan of love for humanity we find the greatest will of our Father for mankind is to accept His Son, Jesus Christ as their personal Lord and Savior, so we might live from the center and bring forth good fruit that is well pleasing to Him. No person may have the spiritual portion of their heart aligned properly if God's love through grace is not placed in them by His Spirit. Jesus is the first born of many siblings and, therefore, He is acutely aware of all that is necessary to think and live from the center. That's why He puts a premium on abiding in His Word so that our Father may show Himself in and through us by His wonderful Holy Spirit. The Holy Spirit's operations are designed to give birth to a new being, open the door of divine compassion to all humanity in the earth through the nine gifts listed in *1 Corinthians 12:7-11*

> *But the manifestation of the Spirit is given to every man to profit withal. For to one is given by the Spirit the word of wisdom; to another the word of knowledge by the same Spirit; To another faith by the same Spirit; to another the gifts of healing by the same Spirit; To another the working of miracles; to another prophecy; to another discerning of spirits; to another divers kinds of tongues; to another the interpretation of tongues: But all these work that one and the selfsame Spirit, dividing to every man severally as he will.*

Whenever we get off center, the Holy Spirit is here gently guiding us back to the place He knows our Heavenly Father wants us to live. In doing this we may fulfill our call. Jesus Christ is the supreme example of center living, center thinking and pure motive of the heart in our Father's vast Kingdom.

Shop all of our books and Christian materials at
www.BOLDTRUTHPUBLISHING.com
For more information contact us
beirep@yahoo.com

www.ingramcontent.com/pod-product-compliance
Lightning Source LLC
Chambersburg PA
CBHW071016040426
42443CB00007B/809